D0041078

BOOKS BY ROD McKUEN

POETRY

AND AUTUMN CAME
STANYAN STREET & OTHER SORROWS
LISTEN TO THE WARM
LONESOME CITIES
TWELVE YEARS OF CHRISTMAS
IN SOMEONE'S SHADOW
CAUGHT IN THE QUIET
A MAN ALONE
(PRINTED IN LIMITED EDITION)
WITH LOVE . . .
FIELDS OF WONDER
THE CAROLS OF CHRISTMAS
MOMENT TO MOMENT
BEYOND THE BOARDWALK
AND TO EACH SEASON . . .

COLLECTED LYRICS

NEW BALLADS
PASTORALE
THE SONGS OF ROD MCKUEN
GRAND TOUR

AND TO EACH SEASON...

and
to each season...

ROD McKUEN

CHEVAL BOOKS
—
SIMON AND
SCHUSTER
—
NEW YORK

Published by Simon and Schuster
Rockefeller Center, 630 Fifth Avenue
New York, New York 10020
and Cheval Books, Box 2783
Los Angeles, California 90028

FIRST PRINTING, SEPTEMBER 1972

SBN 671-21411-X
Library of Congress Catalog Card Number: 72-83893
Manufactured in the United States of America

to the memory of my mother

CONTENTS

and to each season
something is special,
lilacs, red rose
and the white willow.
young men of fortune,
old men forgotten,
green buds renewing
the brown leaves
dead and gone . . .

AUTHOR'S FOREWORD

The Japanese poet Takubuku said, "Every man keeps a prisoner groaning in his heart. . . ." This book is an attempt to free such a prisoner—or more than one—from mine. I am not sure if it succeeds. No one of us, I think, can name, let alone free, those demons—friendly or otherwise—that keep us from being the kind of men we'd like to be.

My childhood, before eleven, remains elusive. I've yet to get it down on paper the way it was. New York is easier to write about and San Francisco writes itself, but Elko, Alamo, Ely and Caliente hardly come at all. Even when my memory has a favored day, some prisoners refuse escape.

My mother, though her death was recent, is hardest of all to fit into words, though she's crowded my head and heart more than anything or anyone this past year.

Physically, in later years she got heavier, mentally, she became—even at the end—more alert. Emotionally, we touched bases without admitting there were bases to be touched. I could paint her, but I cannot yet frame the way she was or is for me in words.

I believe, increasingly, that man is now essentially alone. Irrevocably so. Whether that is good or bad, or can indeed be categorized other than for each case individually, I'm not prepared to say.

For myself, I am grateful for the transients in my life, whether they be Sundays when the phone's not ringing or the odd stranger who happens by and leaves behind more pleasure than my concentration on my own needs quite deserves.

Some of the lines in this book were written nearly twenty years ago and never published; that I loose them now means I find them *true* today. I am more and more concerned with truth, having lied my share within my life, and lately having been a good deal lied about.

I am not convinced the truth can make men free, but I believe it a beginning and a final resting place. Tomorrow, though, I might believe in lies. What I want is not to be held accountable for what I said today, or yesterday, so that my tomorrows can stay open.

Poetry is fact, even in its imagery. This is a work of fact. Any disguise is a defense not known to me as yet. Clouds where clarity should be were not intended. I have not written for every man but I want to write for Everyman, because I wish to be one and the same with all my brothers, yet remain an individual.

That I write so much on love must mean that it is
paramount to me. It is. I have come back from a long
tour just now, having loved nobody and everybody.
This is for me a new beginning, or at least an end.

Rod McKuen

June 11, 1972

WHEN I WAS NINE

1.

When I was nine
or part of nine
we lived in Scamania, Washington.
Our cabin sat beside the highway
so near that we could hear
      cars whiz past us
and trucks grunt up the incline
          late at night.

Behind the house for miles
grew every kind of tree.
My private forest
that another boy
never once walked through.

I'd be sent for firewood
and first come home with flowers
hoping I could please my mother
half as much as I believed
my foster father could.
Never knowing
            and not to know
if wild bouquets made her as happy
as red roses later did.

Because my new found forest
was my own and my own only,
gradually I came to read it
like a scholar poring over books,
muttering to himself at certain passages.
I muttered back at squirrels
and held long dialogues with birds,
fully sure I spoke their language.
Positive their answers
    came in kind.

None ever contradicted me.

2.

It must have been
toward the first of spring
when I first saw him
a mountain lion sleek and soft
pretty as Rousseau might make him,
threading through the wood
padding slow
before he saw me
then stopping as I had
to look me up and down.

Perhaps it was the first time
I had been surveyed
by microscope or microscopic eye.

All that afternoon
we sat not twenty feet apart,
regarding one the other
till he loped off
in search of weasels
or a place of water.
I stayed there still
until the darkness
took the afternoon.
Then I went home,
never speaking of the incident
                    till now.

Thereafter
by unspoken pre-arrangement
he'd follow me
        from house to school
and again from school to house,
remaining always
just outside the clearing,
invisible to anyone but me.
The distance narrowing,
yet still he prowled his private path
and I the man-made trail
where few branches
                gave obstruction
and only now and then
a leaf would rustle
or a twig would snap.

I grew to know
the sorrow in his eyes
though never why;
but ever afterward I sought
that same, soft sadness
in the eyes of strangers
I would have for friends.

Perhaps that's why
my understanding friends are few
they lack a certain sadness
that betrays the truth.

3.

In mid October
the first long rain began
and pings of water
speeding down to pots
from the leaking roof
had turned from pings
                    to plops.

The mud-caulked cabin
that we'd found abandoned
and turned into our summer home
would surely fall that winter,
maybe even with the season's
first hard thrust.

And so we left
even as it rained
determined to be gone
before the snow could catch us.

The model-T had long ago
been traded off
to pay the grocery bill
so now we hitched to California.

My mother with her thumb up
and her pretty smile
got us back down crooked roads
through Washington and Oregon,
along the California coast
and finally to Nevada.

We must have been a spectacle.
                    She out front
as slim as summer,
her husband with my brother
in his arms beside her
and me still looking off behind
hoping I might see
a lion's friendly face.
A sad-eyed lion
pacing out an even pace
keeping his distance,
but being there
in case that one the other
needed one the other.

4.

I wonder if I ever told her
or if my mother ever knew
the first companion
        I called friend
was an animal of gentleness
whose eyes I'll long remember.

Did she know that I had
special dispensation
                and protection?
Or why a lion, not a lamb?

When my family
out of kindness
kidnapped me
and stole me
from my forest friend
they stole my childhood too.

Though I'd still climb trees
and later fell them
as a stopgap on my way to now,
and seek out jungle animals
(and maybe even find a few)
it wouldn't be the same again.

5.

A mountain lion in a forest
is by all accounts
        a curious event,
but he was there.
And written here
between these lines
is what gentleness
        he taught me
and some hardness too,
the way to make my way alone,
though never how to find a friend
and lose him gracefully.

Most of all my lion showed me
that though the forest's
                    padded green
is a different color
from the green of its thick trees
man and lion
          different colors too
can share the same dense jungle
if their eyes have kinship
and they respect the distance
that brings them close.
And the closeness
that insists on distance.

Since that time
when I was nine
        or part of nine,
looking after lions
              has occupied
the front part of my head
and the best part of my time.

No journey's been too far to make
if I thought lions lived there.
And I always look
          from right to left
every time I'm passing
down a new road
              anywhere.

But forests
now fall down around us
the way that autumn rain did
when I was nine in Washington.
And I suppose
what lions there are left
hike the higher hills.
It must be so
for those that prowl
the city pavements
come so seldom anymore
that they can walk
among the populace unnoticed.

THE DAY THEY BUILT THE ROAD

RELIGIOUS EXPERIENCE

The horses would run
down the field
            and scatter.
Let out to pasture
they'd frisk like children
when the bell rings three
and school doors open.

At night
they'd all be back again,
coming to the barn
slow and single file.

When I didn't
chase the horses
     out to pasture
I'd go swimming in the reservoir
off beyond the other side of town,
or sit above a certain pond
tossing pebbles at the water
just to see the circles form,
        widen
and then disappear.

One day coming home
I saw a farmer
pissing by the road.
His balls hung down
        below his hand
and looked so heavy
that I began to run
for no apparent reason.
I didn't stop
until I reached
the safety of my room.

Home again,
I pulled the shade
and got down from the bureau
my Sunday School coloring book.
Having chewed my brown crayola
just the day before,
I had no choice
but to color Jesus Christ's hair
                              yellow.

I made his robes all green
and having no green left
to paint the shrubbery
outlined black
against the stark white sky,
I left it as it was.
The same held true
for all the fishes
and the bread.

On Sunday next
my painting
was the best in class
and to this day
it's still the best one
that I ever colored.

That Sunday
and afterward as well
I started taking
a different road to home
bypassing my favored pond,
not even going near
            the reservoir.

Some time later
I learned to paint
            by numbers
but no one ever cared
as much for anything
I ever colored up
as that first
yellow headed Jesus Christ.

"Inspired," the Deacon said.
Even now it's hanging
                in the rectory.

THE DAY THEY BUILT THE ROAD

All day we saw them coming,
the trucks and truckers,
the caterpillars
      and cat-skinners.
The foremen and the workmen,
the asphalt spreaders
in their dirty black trucks
who ate the green
with more precision
than the sharpest plow.

They'd cut
straight through
the northeast field
a month before.
The steam shovel harvest
lay there still,
        bent up cornstalks
boulders with their shins skinned.
The hide of the earth
split open and quartered.

And now they'd come
to finish off the job
to cut our lives up too.

Thinking about
the dogs I'd chased
down through the yellow corn,
the girls I'd walked
back home along that fence,
mostly the smell of the field
the song of the crows
the rattle of the field mice
on the new turned ground
made me stop watching them.

They were harvesters
and spoilers too
no different from the farmer
in the next field down the road.

Tomorrow
we'd start smelling gasoline
and diesel smoke
as the road
came crashing through.

Mama said,
It's just a road.
But she knew too
that with the coming of the road
our lives would change,
it wouldn't be the same.
And it wasn't.

LEAVING

Some of us were leaving
little towns and pretty places
(though we thought them ugly
             at the time).
That is not to say
that we were special
set apart from those who stayed.
We were movers
    but of our own selves only

Not unlike the cabbage
grown for city market
there came a time to be detached
      and trucked away.
And we went willingly.

Some of us
went away
just to get away
some of us left
because horizons never stop.

Beyond each hill
a new one waits
and pulls us
like the hidden hands
        of love.

Some of us thought
we'd walk a little taller
if we walked away.

Some of us were driven off
some of us went driving off
and there were those
who couldn't do
or wouldn't do
what those who stayed behind
were left to do.

Some of us
chased shadows
        dreams
            ambitions
and as we went
we waved goodbye
            forever.

Some there were
who lived in whistle stops
                now deserted
but for the weekly train.
Some had never seen a train
and thumbed their way
along dirt roads
or slick new WPA highways.

But whether we rode off
in coaches or in cattle cars
or crouched beneath cabooses
shitting railroad ties
that engines up ahead
had only just now eaten,
we were leaving.

Most of us without exception
had no pre-determined destination.
There were jobs in Tonopah
logging to be done outside Seattle
and heading East
            you always came back rich.

Most of all
there was some living
to be done.
Even I knew that,
ever since they built the road.

Mama shrugged
and let me go
with some misgiving,
and I suspect
a little pride.

LESSONS

LESSON: ONE

I leave you on the bed
still within the dark
         genuinely sorry
     that it came to this.
And then the long walk home
and climbing the stairs
to be alone
         and maybe sleep,
   or whatever,
but not to think.

The year twenty gone
I concentrate on twenty-one
and so begin to wonder
                when it is
a man becomes a man.
Will I be officially informed
by the tax man or the rule book maker?

I've noticed that the hair
upon my belly's darkened
and it moves toward my chest,
yet though a forest stands
where only trees once stood
                I don't feel different.

I leave you
          walk away
sorry for the first time.

Tomorrow when you waken
there'll be sun
and you'll forget.
But me,
think how it is for me
not knowing what
the transformation means
or if it's come or will come.

I left you silent in the dark
but I know darkness too.

LESSON: TWO

I'm standing still
behind the window
cut off from the traffic
and the truth by glass.

I do not live within a lie
because I do not live at all.
Perhaps I've found
a kind of purgatory
just before the truth
but if it waits beyond
it's out of sight.

LESSON: THREE

Times there are
to skate across the faces
of street strangers
and times to hang in close.
Passion isn't always the decider
                or it shouldn't be.
As defenses from damnation
should not decide our prayers
so we should be wise enough
to let the stranger have
the say-so sometimes.
Even when the say-so's *no.*

FORT ORD/ OCTOBER, 1953

BASIC TRAINING

Stumbling
      striding
  half running
down the stairs
to stand formation.

Awakened
not by
      just the cadre's whistle
or the threatened roll call
but mostly by the winter morning
hard against our faces.

Still buttoning shirts and
            fumbling with flies,
our piss hard-ons now softened
by the cold October day
we stood the name count
slouched and squint-eyed,
not hearing anything
but one the other's
        stomach grumbling
asleep though standing
each anticipating his own name
and barking back affirmatively
            when it came.

Seven-thirty
and inspection done,
the street again
and ranks of sorts.
Soon a khaki ribbon
unrolling down the road.
Contracting up a hill.
Unrolling down the road.

Another hill
and we passed on
(the road like a conveyor belt
intact from Modern Times).

Then a river
where a girl picked roses.

By now these boy-men
　　　　of six hours ago
seemed too tired
　　　　to even sigh
at the sweet spectacle
of that young girl's
top thighs showing
as she bent low
to cut the roses
nearest to the ground.

I was looking
past the roses
and the rosy thighs
to another hill ahead

CONDITIONING

Does the enemy
that I'll be killing soon
sleep well?
The one who daily trains
to kill his brother, me?

What did he eat
            for breakfast
and was his simulated battle
every bit as dull as mine today?

I hope I see his face.
I hope I learn the name
of every man I kill.
It does seem pointless
to kill anything
without the chance
to hate it first.

INFORMATION

How will we tell
those dead soldiers
and those men dying now
that the war's been won?

Won at tables
by the old men of both sides,
giving this point—
         taking that.
Erasing paragraphs
just as easily as they taught us
how to win lead medals
for erasing lives.

We'll all wake up
as semi-angels
if we wake at all.
The fighting done,
the winning done,
we'll find we chose
the right side after all.
The papers and the radio
will take care
        to tell us that.

The other side
has papers, too,
how fortunate that most of us
have just enough equipment
to understand our own tongues only.

I know I should be grateful
to be fighting and God-fearing
                    on the side of right,
living in *one nation*
indivisible under God.

But I have known some men
                    to wonder
though I've never heard one ask
what the enemy believes in.

STANYAN STREET & BEYOND

STANYAN STREET, 4

There are those times
when I'm not sure
there ever was a house
on Stanyan Street.
That house,
just like that long gone love
    fades, too, sometimes.
One doesn't think
to photograph the *now*
when you're convinced it lasts.

But real it was and is.
And reality for some of us
is only those things
done or thought done
    and well remembered.

ENTR'ACTE

We were in love that summer
and birds about the sky
were singing with themselves,
carols I cannot remember,
though I do recall
            the color of the trees
and the things I thought
but never said to you.

I thought of San Francisco
and the bridge being painted
even when it wasn't Spring.
I thought about
the loneliness of oceans,
of Colorado snow
and writing a book called
                    Where Can I Go.
Everything but us.
We were a fact
and not to be embellished on,
or thought about.

Now I remember
you liked brandy
and Bruckner
          and beer,
and painting Mt. Baker
as it sank into the fog.

You liked little boys
and skipping breakfast
(unless we made it for ourselves).

In that whole season
as warm day followed warm day
I never thought about
tomorrow or next year.
Of course you never do
when it's happening for you,
and it was happening
for both of us.

When did we stumble,
where did we turn
when did we stop
as though we'd never started?

It was, I think,
somewhere near
September's end.
Other people started
getting in between us,
almost as though
we hadn't locked the gate.

Thinking back now
I may have even come upon
an answer to the *why*.

Sometimes being happy
seems a self-indulgence.

When on every side of you
the world seems wrapped in wrong,
it becomes a bending burden
to go on smiling
or to smile at all
even for the one you love.

We had friends
who never laughed,
not because there was a war—
                    there was,
but then there always is.
But fun had lost
a button off its pants,
            the first one,
and none of us were making any effort
to sew it on again.

27 AUGUST, 1971

I know why
your belly's soft,
because so many men
have pressed against it
and into it.
So don't complain at my weight,
for when I come down
hard on you
it will only be
an act of loving
to wipe out all of those
indelible impressions left
by men mightier than me
and younger, yes—
but none who needed
your round belly more.

I shove my life
              deep into yours
until the melting
and the melding
brings us both so close
that cross or crowbar
will remain unable
to divide us.

UP AHEAD

There is nothing
I wouldn't do for you.
There isn't anything
you wouldn't do for me.
So are we to spend our lives
doing nothing for each other?

THE COMING OF THE RAIN

THE COMING OF THE RAIN

It seems as though
the rain has not begun
and yet that it will never stop.

So much love has passed between us
that we've made our own rain
as we've made the afternoon
last through half the night
by moving back and forth
across each other
again and time again.

I'd love to fill you to the brim
so that you'd be always full
                    and spilling over,
then I could know for sure
no interloper however tall
weaving through the distance
would find shelter in you
from the next November rain
or hide your body
from the long
September shadows
          with his own.

And still it rains
as though the sky's let go
                for always.
A thoughtful rain
as I go back to bed
and you go off
to make a chocolate cake.

The rain that I had damned
                all morning,
I bless tonight.
Don't wake me if I fall asleep
even if your fist
        is full of frosting.

ABSOLUTES

How true is truth
          how absolute?
If I say love
do I mean loving you
to the intrusion of all else
and of all others?
And do I know
if I mean that?

There are wild roses
that have bloomed
        far into December,
seemingly without a reason.
And some faithful trees
stay barren all year long.
Proving, I suppose,
the only thing consistent
        is inconsistency.

Let me say
I will not lie to you
and know I'm lying.
Nor will I comfort you
in any false way
however expedient that may seem.

And if I catch myself pretending
I'll tell on me
however much it hurts.

Fall down
with me, for now
and let me prove to you
how much I love
inside out and outside in.
If you're still afraid
then guide me if you like.
I love your hand
as much as I love
what's inside your heart.

SANTA MONICA SUMMER, 3

Chasing down the beach for grunion
                    after midnight
                         finding none
            but stumbling over one another.
        on the way back home.
Part of another
Santa Monica summer
when all went well
            or did it ?
Perspectives, like horizons, change.

The facts are these,
I loved you
I meant to always be there
just as I meant to master algebra
somewhere along the line.
The line grew shorter
as the shadows all
grow longer now.

The need for algebra
began to fade
        as surely
as the need for you
grew stronger
and grows stronger still
now that you're away.

I did not intend to master you
but I wish I'd taken time
to learn more than your body.

That geography,
though dear enough to me,
was as incomplete
without the doorway
of your mind ajar
as a midnight hunt for grunion
several summers back
              in Santa Monica.

APRIL POEMS, 1971/1972

IOWA FROM AN AIRPLANE

Above Iowa and looking down
the patchwork quilt of farms
unfolding through the oval window.
Now short green squares,
now broad gray triangles
and oblong stretches
of fresh-turned chocolate earth
that surveyors would find hard
                    to pace off.
Plots and pleats of land
orphaned from a quilting bee.

Though mid April grapples
        with the middle earth
bare trees still stand bare.
Airports are the only eyesore
as silos dot and red barns dash
           the land,
and God plays bridge
with unseen friends
and shows the world his hand.

Tractors track the squares
and fences follow
every crooked line
they helped create,
though even fences
make no boundary lines
and Iowa in the eye seems full enough
to spill across the continent
if not across the world.

APRIL MAN

An April evening
tangled in the river's tail
whining of itself
as the wind does
in the eaves
      of broken buildings.

Crickets—if they are crickets
sound like seagulls
      or the crackling fire
as every bit of life there is
is trapped above the river
              or below.

I am not signaling
for May to come
nor tapping out
           a message
to the ears of June.
I'm held in place
and helpless,
like a given April night
the tail of some brown river
still holds on to.

I've brought you
nothing new
nor can I lead you
through tomorrow.
But if you travel back
to where I am
I'll let you stroke the tail
of my brown river
or wrap your naked limbs
around your battered brother
who has given in
but still remains
an April man.

FREEDOM

Free I am.
I have no bills to pay.
My debts are squared,
the edges smoothed out
                    perfectly.
My ducks are in a row
           and I can sail.

But there are borders
in this final life
that were not here
          at nineteen
or at twenty-three
I'll not admit
that I erected them
or even that I helped.

What if I did
not even knowing
what I built
with my erector set?

I am not accountable

My new found freedom
only came just now
and I'm experimenting
with it still.

Happily there's no one left
                to disappoint
if I should stumble
        in the dark
or die while diving
through a dream
that didn't end.

To those who'd jail me
let them try.
My boundaries
        and responsibilities,
if they were ever there,
now blur into a single
tie-dyed day.

SLEEP AFTER THE BRIGHTON LANES

Saturday night
ducking, dodging
through the Brighton lanes,
pursuing and pursued.

When nothing comes
of conquest or conquistador
the quietude of that same
upstairs room
is like an iron mantle
clamping down and making
every organ useless.

And still sleep doesn't come.

It's then you know
that speech is nothing.
                    Not because
there is no one to speak to
but because yet one more time
you were not chosen
by the chosen
and you did not choose
                    to speak
even though the chosen
might have waited
thinking your words
should come first.

Why do we study,
Why do we become
        learned men?
Why do we cheat
            and force
and push our way
through what we think
are barricades,
when all the while
it is those same
blind barrioadoo
that we're erecting?

When it comes to need
intellect could not be
                more useless
and there's not knowledge
near enough or deep enough
to satisfy or substitute.

With imagination so well worn
that a single sigh is every bit
as powerful as sublimation.
Need can drive you
down the darkest alley
and leave you there,
beached and bloody,
still waiting for
a new encounter.

Need,
and need not gratified
has helped me understand
why the suicide can do it
and how the alcoholic can
transcend and thereby end
                    his limit.

Monday morning,
out of sleep,
too little sleep
that came too late.
The car is waiting.
On to Bournemouth.

Another night of faces
not seen completely
        and not seen again.
There are eyes and forms
that stand out even in the dark.
They become then individuals
                not audience.
They never know
and I can't tell them.

What if I put the question
to some of those who linger
when the show shuts down
and the answer came back, *no?*

One more bed
in one more room
now sleep hurries in,
even though the senses
still stay poised
for the small
or great adventure.
Tomorrow there's the London train,
a month to go
and then Los Angeles again.

LILAC STRAIN

There is a lilac strain
that runs the breadth of England
and yet no bloom is more maligned.

Superstition says that death
lurks within the house
that houses them.
And so the bower
      and the bush
are left untouched.

Their blooms not plundered
and sold like daffodils.
Their branches never amputated
and trucked to town
like the early blooms
              of fruit trees.
Lilacs of all colors
stay protected from the vase
              and florist's visit—
for that one short month
that ends the Spring.

MR. KELLY, JR.

The dog's eyes
never close at night.
Is he guarding me
or grieving me?
Does he worry of the known
or of the unknown?

I've no need to muzzle time
         and anyway,
it's running at a pace
I couldn't catch
or stay abreast of
even with the help of Mercury.

THE HERMIT CRAB

As I watch you
move beyond the door
I remember that some oceans
have been known to come again
to their mother country
and wash ashore
more brilliant treasures
than they took away.

It is small comfort
to a man who lately
greets each season
as the hermit crab
hides in the rocks
and scurries from intruders
be they from the land or sea.

MOTHER'S DAY

There are so many lilacs
in southern Ohio
these last days of April
and these first days of May
that I could fill up
all your rooms with them
if you were still alive to smell
and still alive to fill for me
that void your dying opened up.

It's spring, and Mother's Day.
How I wish that April death
had caught us both together.

Today I felt so far away
from you and California
and from what I thought life was
that these may surely be
the last full lilac days
I'll ever know.

I wish to be remembered
remembering Ohio lilac trees
that blossomed in the spring you died.

MAMA & LITTLE JOE

THE LEAVING OF LITTLE JOE

Cats know.
They're as good
as bank clerks
     at sensing
loss or gain,
better than the clergy
or the clairvoyant
at seeing up ahead.
And in the dark
they're more at home
than any ghost.

One year
to the day
that Mama died
Joe turned up missing.
    He was Mama's cat
more than all the others.
He had grieved with us
and been estranged from us
since that Easter night
         a year ago
when Mama's clothes
         came home.

At first
he stalked the house,
not satisfied to prowl
        only her own rooms.
Finally sure that she was gone
and not in hiding,
he began to talk to each of us,
and then to scold us all
        as if we were to blame
            for her long absence.

One by whiskered one
he finally took on
all the other cats
        till none
would venture near him.

Cats are deliberate.
Nothing that they do
is done by chance.
Whether making love
or making conversation
they work in earnest
for earnestness is all the work
                    they do.
Ed says that when the time comes
cats go off to die alone.
We looked everywhere,
but didn't look for long.
Joe stayed away,
and all the other cats
                    came back.

In retrospect
there's always been
a cat or two in transit
moving in and being loved,
then leaving at his own volition.
Playing, if it pleased him
            preening if it didn't.

Cats that helped us show
the better sides of ourselves
            to each other
or anyway, the calmer one.
It didn't start with Sloopy
and it won't end with Little Joe.

Once Billy found an old Tom
we nicknamed A Marvelous Cat.
                    I believe he was,
though why I can't remember.

Currently, there's Paco the Brave
                    and Greta,
Charlie with the mustache
Squeek who talks
along the hallway
announcing himself as he enters
                    every room.

Nickoli and Odyssey I leave out.
They're merely kittens
and kittens as you know
are not exactly cats.

And Nuisance.
Nuisance is the loner.
She dines with Mr. Kelly
                every night.
She doesn't like most other cats
and bites to signal
when she's tired of being petted,
by even those of us
she knows are friends.
She comes to eat
but sleeps in someone else's yard
                   or wherever.

Paco, on the other hand,
prefers to be with Eddie
and wanders slow about the house,
his tail long and dragging,
every time that Eddie goes away.

But when Helen
or good company
            comes into town
that tail's straight up and fanning.
He even cleans himself in private
before beginning to show off
his plumage and his Valentino stare.

Greta's friends with everyone.
At the moment she's curled up
            on my left foot.
Instead of moving to get comfortable,
      I indulge her
just as I did all the other cats
who came and went throughout the years.

Nuisance will be next to go
for she loved Mama, too,
and lately she has started sitting
            outside Mama's room
as if to guard it.
She bares her teeth
at all who travel by.

Knowing cats
we all know what to make of it.

Cats, when ready leave at night.
Or maybe it's the daytime.
One is never sure because
            before they're gone
each has managed to become a habit
as comfortable as any well loved child
or a piece of furniture.
They turn up missing
only when you've time
            to miss them.

Little Joe must have known
we cared for him as much
                as Mama did.
He should have given us a chance.
But cats are not like anything
                but cats.
You don't choose them.

With any luck at all
a cat will come along
                and fancy you
for his duration, not your own.

If I thought
that cats were anything
            but deliberate,
I'd bolt the door on Nuisance.
But I do believe
that she's determined.

After all
she's given us
a full six years
of her precious time.

She's entitled to be rid of us
if that's her choice.

ABOUT THE AUTHOR

ROD McKUEN *was born in Oakland, California, and has traveled extensively throughout the world both as a concert artist and a writer. In less than five years six of his books of poetry have sold nearly eight million copies in hard cover, making him the best-selling and most widely read poet of all times. In addition he is the best-selling living author writing in any hard-cover medium today. His poetry is taught and studied in schools, colleges, universities and seminaries throughout the world, and the author spends a good deal of his time visiting and lecturing on campus.*

Mr. McKuen is also the composer of more than 1,000 songs that have been translated into Spanish, French, Dutch, German, Russian, Czechoslovakian, Japanese, Chinese, Norwegian and Italian, among other languages. They account for the sale of more than one hundred million records. His film music has twice been nominated for Motion Picture Academy Awards.

Rod McKuen's classical music, including symphonies, concertos, piano sonatas and his very popular Adagio for Harp & Strings, is performed by leading orchestras in the United States and throughout Europe. In May of 1972, the Royal Philharmonic Orchestra in London premiered his Concerto #3 for Piano & Orchestra, and an orchestral suite, The Plains of My Country.

Before becoming a best-selling author and composer, Mr. McKuen worked as a laborer, radio disc jockey and newspaper columnist. Of his military service during and after the Korean War, the author says, "I was a private in the army who rose from that rank once only to descend rather swiftly."

The author makes his home in California in a rambling Spanish house which he shares with a menagerie of Old English sheep dogs and seven cats. He likes outdoor sports and driving. He has just completed an extensive book about the sea and is currently editing and assembling the first definitive collection of the words and music to more than fifty of his most popular songs. Both books will be published by Simon and Schuster.

The complete text to the song "and to each season . . ." is contained in the Stanyan Records album "The Carols of Christmas," and excerpted in the Warner Bros. album "Odyssey."

HB9C